D0450025

The Fun Book

102 Ways for Girls to Have Some

Melina Gerosa

Illustrations by Melanie Marder Parks

SIMON & SCHUSTER

Simon & Schuster
SIMON & SCHUSTER
Rockefeller Center
1230 Avenue of the Americas
New York, NY 10020

Designed by Karolina Harris

Manufactured in the United States of America

3 5 7 9 10 8 6 4 2

Library of Congress Cataloging-in-Publication Data
Gerosa, Melina.
The fun book: 102 ways for girls to have some / Melina Gerosa; illustrations by Melanie Marder Parks.
p. cm.
1. Women—Life skills guides—Miscellanea. 2. Women—Psychology—Miscellanea. 3. Spontaneity (Personality trait) 4. Lifestyles.
I. Title.
HQ1221.G44 1998
158'.082—dc21 97-40747 CIP
ISBN 0-684-84398-6

For Jennifer

INTRODUCTION

BACK in my high school days—a time when Lionel Ritchie ruled the airwaves, when Molly Ringwald was It, and when leg-warmers were actually cool—something devastating happened to me. I was stood up. Not just by any geek but by my A-list crush. By a guy whom I was positive was The One. There I was, lurking behind the upstairs bathroom window, primped and primed in my cutest date outfit, naming our children. Then the minutes turned into hours, and the hours turned into the horrifying realization that I had been blown off, big time.

One phone call later, my best friend Karen screeched into my driveway in her parents' beat-up MG convertible. Although it was November, the top was down and the heat was blasting. Karen flung open the door, handed me a blanket, and off we roared into the night.

First stop, Baskin-Robbins for double scoops of my favorite flavor, Pralines and Cream. Cones in gloved hands, we cruised around town as I copiloted the radio. After a few songs, I station-surfed right into Carly Simon's "Anticipation." Thrilled, we cranked up the volume and belted out every word. The people we passed looked at us as if we were crazy, but before I knew it (and despite the fact that my love life was lying in ruins before me), I was enjoying myself.

That was fifteen years ago, and I can still remember the delight of the wind in my hair, the power of Carly's lament, and the creamy taste of that cone. But, ironically enough, I can't even recall my phantom date's name. That's because something important happened to me that evening: I discovered the Divine Power of Fun. It rescued me, and at the age of seventeen, I learned one of life's sweetest secrets: Fun can be the knight in shining armor that never lets me down, even when Prince Charming does.

Ever since that fateful night, I've taken fun seriously. And I've learned a thing or two about it along the way. Fun is the verb of joy. Fun makes an ordinary moment spontaneously combust into pleasure. Fun pops out from the bland backdrop of dull routine like a sunny bouquet of wildflowers arriving from a secret admirer.

Planned or spontaneous, fun is the fabric of happy memories, the icing on the cake of life. Fun keeps you living in the moment. All problems of the past and future worries are—at least temporarily—banished from the kingdom. Just ask the brokenhearted seventeen-year-old girl I was then: Fun is possible anytime, anywhere—especially when you least expect it.

That's because fun rebels. It loves nothing better than to break the rules. Fun is all nerve and no pride. Inappropriately, it sneaks in where it's not invited. This I learned during the tension-filled weeks of final exams in college. Bored for the moment with oceanography's convection currents, some studymates and I went off in search of brain food: chocolate M&M's. Ambling back from the local convenience store, we took a shortcut through the football field. There, on the fifty-yard line, we sat in a circle designing one another's futures. We spared no detail of the exciting career, the gorgeous apartment, and, of course, the adoring husband that awaited each one of us. We concluded our field trip with a pact: We all had to make out with a classmate on that exact spot at least once before graduation day.

While that evening did not exactly secure me a place in the echelons of oceanography, it did teach me two other lessons about fun. First of all, it can invade the most exclusive stress-fest at the slightest provocation. And second, fun, like love, grows exponentially when shared. A budding friendship blooms better with the help of a hearty laugh, a shared secret, and a good time.

Fun is also the ultimate gift you can give yourself. Stop the world's worst day dead in its tracks and do something special, something irresponsible, something just for you. Once, in the throes of the midweek blahs, I wandered into the uncharted territory of the Bergdorf Goodman's couture department. I'd often passed the store to "visit" the dresses in the window, but that day I ventured inside to peek at the price tags. The next thing I knew I was admiring myself in the three-way mirror, in backless, floor-length black satin splendor! And inquiring about matching shoes, no less! About eight outfit changes and two hours later, I ended my afternoon of playing big girl Barbie doll with a "Thanks. I'll think about it."

Trying on unaffordable clothes may not be everyone's idea of a grand time. Still, I think Holly Golightly, heroine of *Breakfast at Tiffany's,* was onto something when she elevated fun to an art form. Immortalized by Audrey Hepburn in the classic 1961 film, Holly donned tiaras, dared her dates to try new things, and audaciously asked Tiffany's to engrave a trinket. In short, she treated life as one continuous cocktail party.

Which brings me to the most important point: Fun doesn't depend on money or stature or the circumstances of your life. Fun is a state of mind. It's driving a convertible with the top down in the winter. It's chocolate-flavored group procrastination. It's playing dress-up no matter what your age.

But seeing the world through Holly Golightly's fabulous Givenchy sunglasses isn't always so easy. Life can get complicated for the woman who wants it all. Entire days are spent crossing chores off the list: trudge to work, pick up the dry cleaning, rush to the gym, pay the bills, return phone calls, go to sleep, wake up, and hit the rewind button. But among the things you *should* do, are an infinite number of things you *could* do.

On these next pages I offer you my personal collection of "coulds," my favorite ideas for how to stop the routine and celebrate life. Ever since that night when I waited dateless, a damsel in distress by the bathroom window, fun has chivalrously picked me up and carried me away. So now, dear reader, let me introduce you to that knight in shining armor. Fun knows how to show a girl a good time.

Take care of the luxuries, and the necessities will take care of themselves.

—DOROTHY PARKER

CELEBRATE the first day of summer by giving yourself a fire-engine-red pedicure. Click down the street in a pair of open-toe mules, platform sandals, or Dr. Scholl's.

KISS someone . . .

- ★ on top of the Empire State Building
- ★ on a chairlift
- ★ while slow dancing in the back of a New Orleans blues bar
- ★ in a leaf pile
- ★ as you drive over the Golden Gate Bridge
- ★ after doing a tequila shot in Acapulco
- ★ in a gondola
- ★ on a trampoline
- ★ in the penguin house at the zoo
- ★ under a gazebo during a lightning storm
- ★ under the stars at the bottom of the Grand Canyon
- ★ on his boss's desk

- ★ while two-stepping in a country-western bar
- ★ on a bed of petals
- ★ while flying first class over international waters
- ★ on home plate at Wrigley Field
- ★ behind the book stacks in the library
- ★ in a eucalyptus forest
- ★ under water
- ★ in black tie, anytime, anywhere.

Make sure to keep track.

USE your meanest ex-boyfriend's T-shirt to clean the bathroom.

BUY a cheap pair of big Jackie O. sunglasses. Pretend that you are incognito.

We all live in suspense, from day to day, from hour to hour; in other words, we are the hero of our own story.

—MARY MCCARTHY

THE next time you're feeling depressed, bake gingerbread people cookies in the shapes of people you know. Deliver them to the people you like. Bite off the heads of the ones you don't. Here's the recipe:

GINGERBREAD CRUNCH THERAPY

Prep time: 1 hour plus chilling

3½ cups all-purpose flour
1 tablespoon pumpkin pie spice
1 teaspoon baking soda
1 teaspoon salt
¼ pound (1 stick) butter, softened
¾ cup packed brown sugar
1 large egg
½ cup light molasses

Combine the flour, pumpkin pie spice, baking soda, and salt in a bowl. Beat the butter and sugar with an electric mixer at medium-high speed until light and fluffy. Beat in the egg and molasses. With the mixer at low speed, add the dry ingredients just until blended. Divide the dough into quarters and flatten into disks. Wrap and refrigerate for 4 hours or overnight, until firm.

Heat the oven to 350 degrees. Grease 2 large cookie sheets. On a floured surface with a floured rolling pin, roll 1 disk ⅛ inch thick. Cut out shapes with gingerbread man and woman cookie cutters. Transfer to the cookie sheets. Bake 8 to 10 minutes, until the edges are lightly browned. Cool on the pans for 1 minute, then transfer to wire racks. Roll and cut the remaining dough until your sources of inspiration have run out.

MAKES 7 DOZEN

THE next time you feel sad for no reason, put The Who's "Love Reign O'er Me" in your Walkman. Turn up the volume and go out for a walk, ideally on a windy, stormy day. Now pretend that there are movie cameras filming you in your exquisite state of devastation. Cry, if possible, and imagine that your lover, the dashing Russian prince, who also happened to be a spy, was killed defending your honor. Remind yourself that your heart is breaking! Think of the priceless diamond and sapphire bracelet that went down in the plane with him, never to be seen again! As you are returning to shelter, imagine the director's arm around your shoulder. He is whispering that you are exquisitely talented. Better than Meryl! More beautiful than Julia! Hollywood is already buzzing about your Oscar nomination! Now imagine that your leading man is lounging in your trailer with a box of Godiva chocolates. If this doesn't cheer you up, simply rewind and repeat.

BUY a medium-size pair of cubic zirconia earrings. When someone asks where you got them, sigh deeply, roll your eyes, and answer, "It's a really long story."

LEARN how to make the perfect martini. (James Bond, eat your heart out!) Don't even think about starting unless you have the proper glass (a martini is not a martini in a paper cup!).

1. Fill the glass with ice water and let stand.
2. Fill a small pitcher or a martini shaker (available in most houseware shops for about $30) with ice and four ounces of top-shelf gin. (Note: Vodka may be substituted, but don't expect respect from the true professionals.)
3. Shake or stir vigorously.
4. Discard the ice water and add a half-capful of dry vermouth to the now-chilled glass. Swirl it around so the inside of the glass is now lined with vermouth. Shake out the excess into the sink.
5. Add the chilled gin and two plump green olives. Don't drive, dance.

The reward of a thing well done is to have done it!
—RALPH WALDO EMERSON

MAKE a list of things you want to do someday: own a Chanel suit, make a man weep, run down a Tahitian beach. Post it on your refrigerator or bulletin board with the grocery list.

Imagination is the highest kite one can fly.
—LAUREN BACALL

OWN a pair of broken-in red tag Levi's jeans. Steal them from your brother, boyfriend, or best male friend if possible; if not, buy an un-prewashed pair. (Any army/navy surplus store should have them.) Don't even dream of wearing them in public until the dark, stiff denim gives way to periwinkle perfection. Impatient types can cheat by exploring vintage clothing shops.

FREQUENT dive bars. Play the jukebox and get to know the clientele. Then impress your dates when you take them there for a nightcap. (Dump them if they don't get it.)

PEDRO'S

VISIT that special piece of clothing or jewelry you have fallen in love with but can't yet afford. Try it on periodically to see if the two of you are truly compatible. Decide to commit to a savings plan or hope your crush will fade.

LEARN the art of giving by surprising a friend with a simple present—a bakery cookie, a note card with the image of her favorite dog on it, a gift certificate for two cups at Starbucks. Don't wait for an occasion; give it just because you thought of the person.

To be able to find joy in another's joy: that is the secret to happiness.
—GEORGES BERNANOS

SPLURGE on a pair of expensive sunglasses. Tie a silk scarf around your head. Beg, borrow, or steal a convertible, yank down the top, and go.

The dream is always running ahead.... To catch up, to live for a moment, in unison with it—that is the miracle.

—Anaïs Nin

BUY yourself one exquisite crystal wineglass each Valentine's Day, no matter what the circumstances. As your collection grows, invite one guest per wineglass to share a Valentine's Day drink and observations.

PLAN a living room picnic with your significant other. Unplug the phone, light candles in tall candlesticks, and order in pizza. Spread out a blanket and dine on the floor while listening to Frank Sinatra (if you're feeling romantic) or Barry White (if you're feeling *really* romantic).

IF a friend is traveling, leave messages so the red light on her hotel phone is always blinking.

NAME an angel and imagine that she is watching over you. She can be anyone—a fairy godmother or your beloved late grandmother. Ask her for advice (but not out loud).

BLAST opera (Delibes's *Lakmé* will do the trick) and make my grandmother Lolee's spaghetti sauce. When the neighbors call to complain about the music, invite them over for dinner.

Lolee's Luscious Tomato Sauce

1¼ pounds pork spareribs
1¼ pounds hot Italian sausage links
1 (28-ounce) can tomato puree
1 (28-ounce) can crushed tomatoes
1 (28-ounce) can peeled whole tomatoes
Salt and pepper to taste
2 cloves garlic, crushed
¼ cup red wine
1 large carrot, whole

Brown the meat. Place all the ingredients in a pot and bring to a boil. Turn the heat to low, cover, and simmer for 2 to 3 hours, stirring often.

When the sauce has finished cooking, put the pot in the refrigerator until the next day. Serve over your favorite pasta, accompanied by a fresh green salad sprinkled with Gorgonzola cheese, a warm loaf of Tuscan bread, and many bottles of Chianti wine. Don't forget to put bowls of ricotta cheese and freshly grated Parmesan cheese on the table for family-style, à la mode decadence.

Serves six

BUY an elegant beaded antique top from a vintage clothing shop and wear it with your favorite pair of black pants. When you don your glamorous hand-me-down, imagine its presence at fabulous parties in times past.

HAVE a tea party for three—proper Anglophile attire required. Brew loose tea, and serve with a silver strainer. Use your best paper-thin china, and serve scones with jam and clotted cream.

LEARN the art of the wink.

Fate keeps on happening.
—ANITA LOOS

REMEMBER when you were six and a half? Surprise friends by celebrating their *half* birthdays for a change. Send a birthday card cut in half or give half a present —for example, one salt or pepper shaker, or a single candlestick. Give the other half on the person's real birthday.

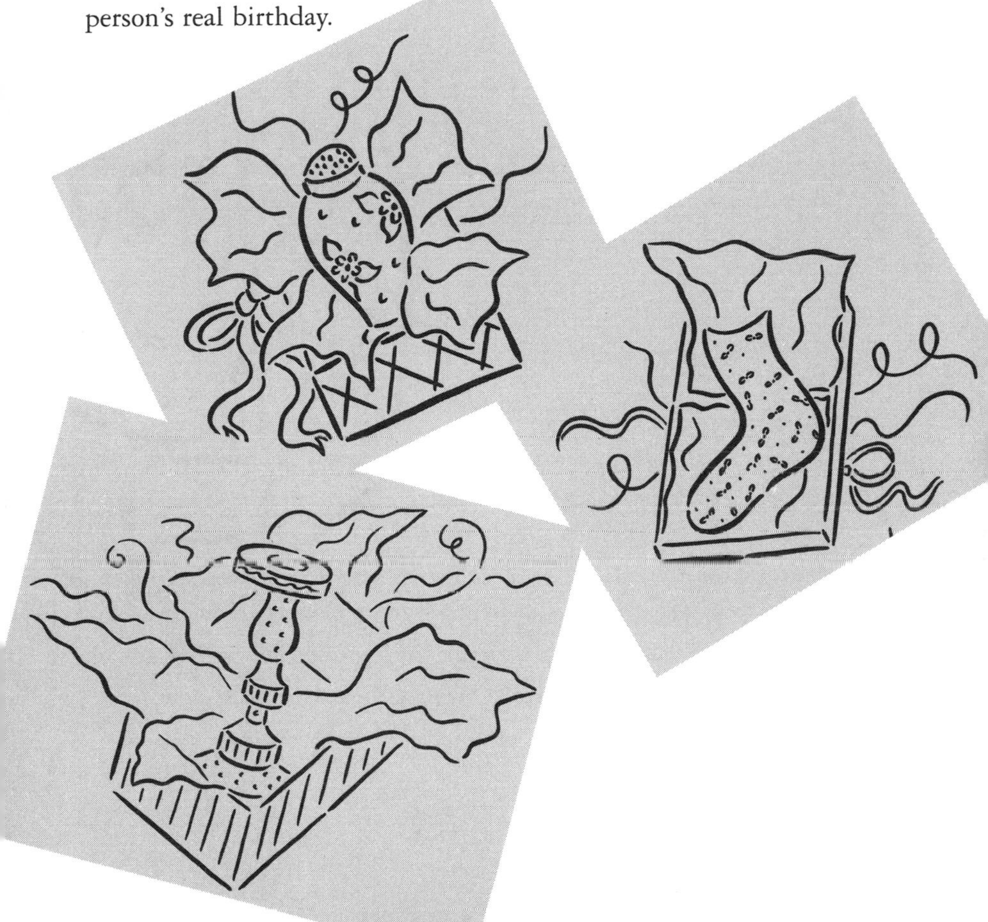

HAVE a Spa Saturday with a friend: Go to the drugstore and introduce each other to your favorite scrubs, masks, and moisturizers. Return home and spend the day on low-cost self-improvement.

SEND roses to a man.

The trouble is, if you don't risk anything, you risk even more.

—ERICA JONG

MAKE a date with a favorite painting at a museum. Spend no less than half an hour getting to know it. See who comes by.

Art is the only way to run away without leaving home.
—TWYLA THARP

INDULGE in big blocks of lemon-scented olive oil soap imported from the south of France. Store in a sweater drawer until you're ready to use them.

REMEMBER, life is one long variety show. You are the star, and your contract demands that you wear as wide a range of clothes as your closet holds. Always court invitations requiring formal attire, and don't be afraid to get dressed up—even if you have no place to go.

WAKE UP in the T-shirt he went to bed wearing.

TUCK lottery tickets inside birthday cards.

HOST the ultimate wine-tasting party. Invite all your friends to bring a vintage from the year they were born and a friend you don't know.

KIDNAP a friend for lunch. Chances are if you show up, she'll drop everything and go—at least for a soda break.

THE next time it snows, put on a Walkman, find a classical station, and go for a run.

MAKE an appointment with a personal shopper at a department store. (The service is free, and they know the merchandise!) Sweep into the store as if you already own it.

GET a massage from someone who doesn't expect one in return.

BUY a pair of very puffy white terry cloth slippers (under $10 at any discount mart).

INVITE your girlfriends over for a sexy salad night. Make sure they come equipped with their favorite bottle of red wine and their most audacious sexual tale. Remember, whoever shares the most entertaining tale wins Sexiest Girl title until the next session. (Believe it or not, this can be far more enlightening than a book club!) You'll impress them with the salad:

SEXY SALAD

Serves 8

chicken breasts, boned, skinned, and split
1 head romaine lettuce, chopped
5 cups mesclun greens
1 pint mushrooms, sliced
1 red pepper, diced
1 package Parmesan-flavored croutons
1 pint cherry tomatoes, split
1 medium Bermuda onion, thinly sliced
11 ounces goat cheese

DRESSING

½ cup olive oil
½ cup balsamic vinegar
1 tablespoon Dijon mustard
Salt and pepper to taste

Grill the chicken. Toss together the lettuce, greens, mushrooms, pepper, tomatoes, and onion.

Mix the dressing ingredients together and toss with the salad.

Place the warm grilled chicken, along with generous blobs of goat cheese, on top. Sprinkle with croutons.

Serve with warm baguettes and let the stories roll.

KEEP a bottle of good champagne in the fridge, just in case. If a good reason doesn't present itself, create one and drink it.

IN honor of the first day of spring, transform your bedroom into an all-white pristine palace. Splurge on Battenberg lace pillow shams and sprinkle lavender-scented powder on pure Egyptian cotton sheets.

ON the night of the first snowfall, light a pine-scented candle and slip into a bubble bath. Decide to believe in Santa and make a wish list.

MEMORIZE your all-time favorite Pablo Neruda poem or Shakespeare sonnet.

LEARN how to make the ultimate toast for any occasion: rehearsal dinners, birthdays, weddings, anniversaries, promotions.

You must do the thing you think you cannot do.
—ELEANOR ROOSEVELT

WHEN visiting a new city, have one drink at the fanciest hotel in town. The people-watching will be on the house. Some of the good ones:

- Aspen: The Little Nell
- Buenos Aires: Alvear Palace
- Chicago: The Drake
- Dallas: The Mansion on Turtle Creek
- Hong Kong: The Peninsula Hotel
- London: The Hempel
- Los Angeles: Four Seasons Hotel at Beverly Hills
- Madrid: The Ritz
- Miami: Delano Hotel
- Milan: The Grand Hotel Et de Milan
- Monte Carlo: Hôtel de Paris
- New Orleans: The Soniat House
- New York: St. Regis
- Palm Beach: The Breakers
- Paris: Le Bristol Hotel
- Rome: Hotel Hassler
- San Francisco: The Fairmont Hotel
- Singapore: Raffles Hotel
- Tokyo: Imperial Hotel
- Venice: Hotel Gritti Palace

CREATE a warm working environment when you are paying bills, writing letters, and getting organized at home by burning a scented candle at your desk. Lemon and lavender reduce stress, vanilla enhances concentration, and green apple helps suppress appetite.

YOU shop. He cooks.

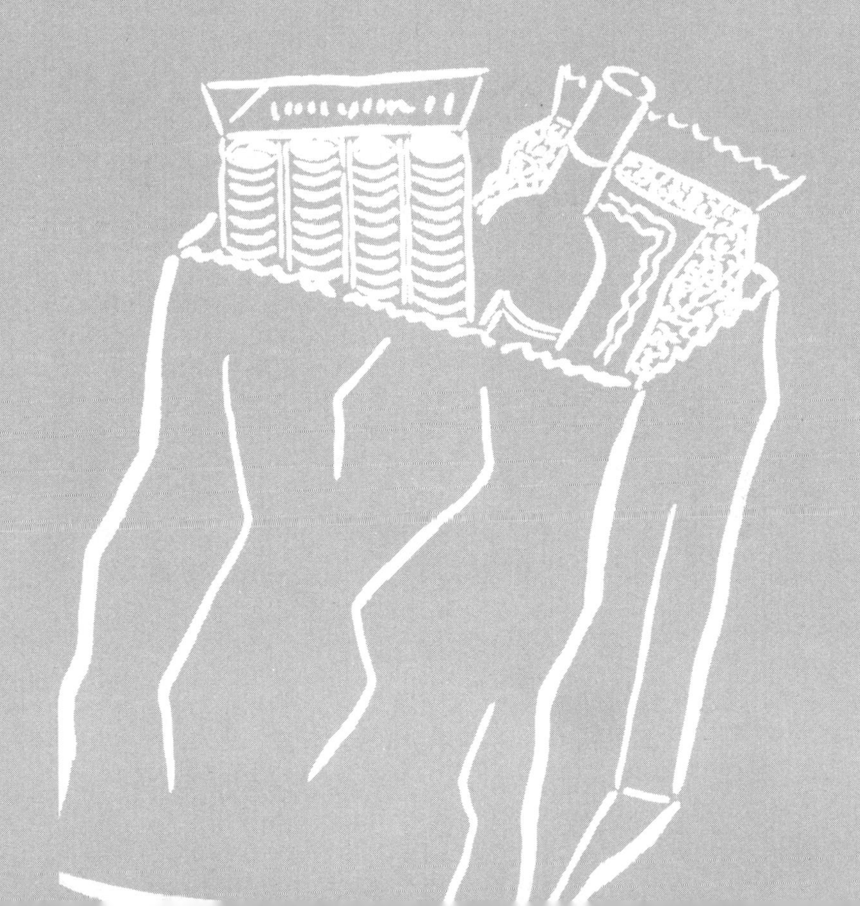

SPEND a day shopping with a friend. Make a pact to buy the same thing: a lipstick, a new sweater, a little spring dress. Buy it for each other and go have cappuccino to celebrate.

REMEMBER the child in you. Gain perspective by eating a peanut butter and jelly sandwich with alphabet soup. Reflect on who you were then and compare with who you have become.

BOOK a $99 flight and go somewhere you've never been for the weekend. Bring carry-on luggage only.

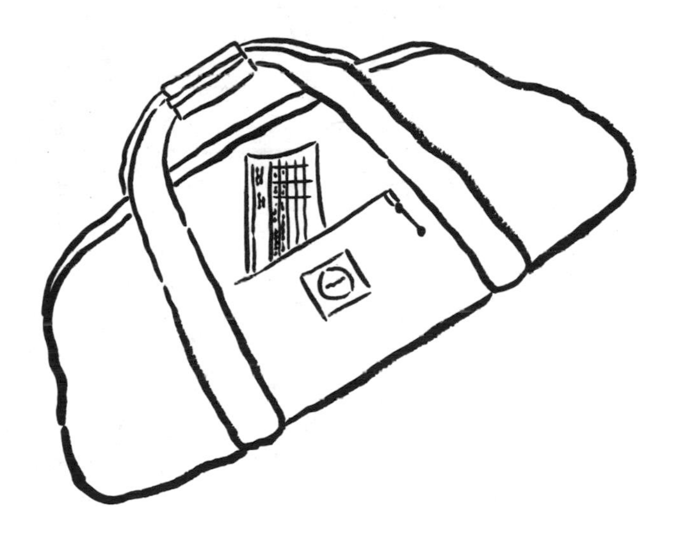

RENT a limousine with six friends and go barhopping. Don't forget to bring along your favorite mixed tape, a cooler of imported beer, and a camera.

KEEP a running list of all the things that make you laugh out loud. Think of them in inappropriate situations, such as religious ceremonies and uptight business meetings.

LEARN how to dance the salsa, tango, or flamenco. Practice in private and surprise your friends the next time you hit the dance floor. Lie and say your grandmother was a professional exotic dancer.

PICK a volume of poetry or a special book and find someone to read it aloud to you, *Little Women*–style.

BEFORE stowing your heavy coat in the back of the closet, tuck $20 in the pocket as next winter's first surprise.

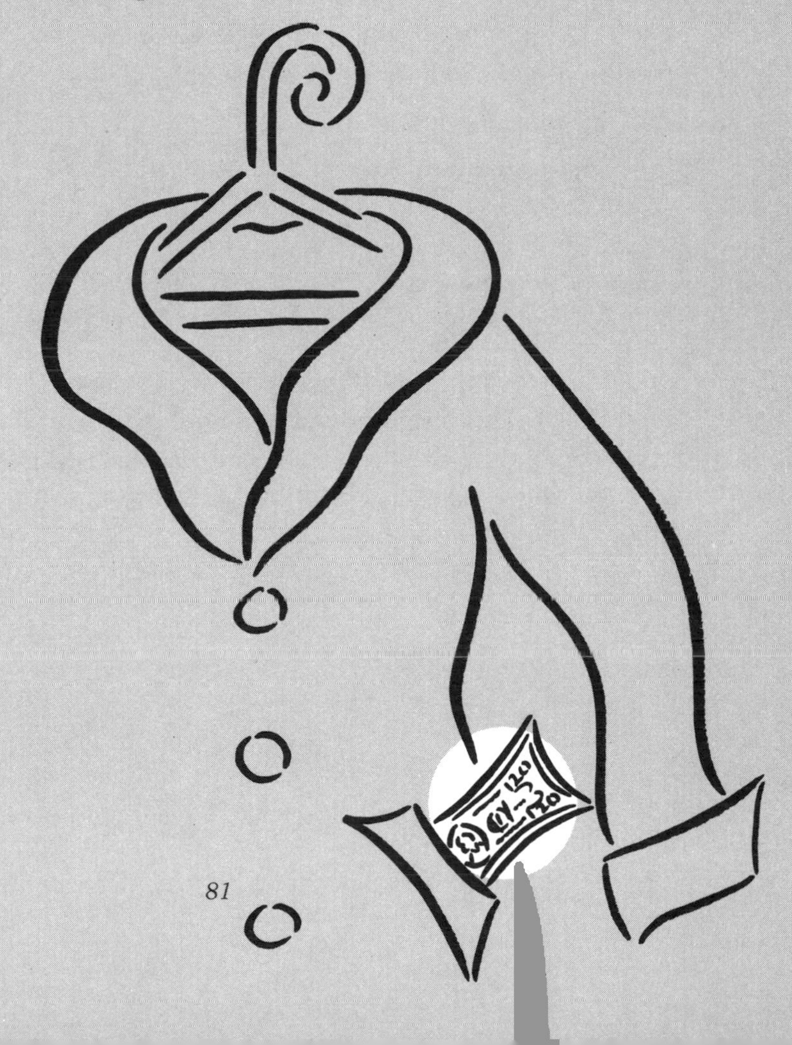

Loco Cocoa

ORGANIZE an ice-skating party. Afterward, drink hot cocoa that you've made from scratch. You'll need:

Five friends
⅓ cup unsweetened cocoa
⅓ cup sugar
4 cups milk
Many marshmallows
Whipped cream

In a medium saucepan, combine the cocoa, sugar, and ½ cup of milk. Cook and stir over medium heat until the mixture starts to boil. Stir in the remaining milk and heat through. Do not boil. Top with marshmallows and whipped cream. Sit back and reflect on Dorothy Hamill's haircut.

EVERY year on Groundhog Day, skip work and make a date with a girlfriend to buy special lingerie. Stealth-dress; wear it under blue jeans.

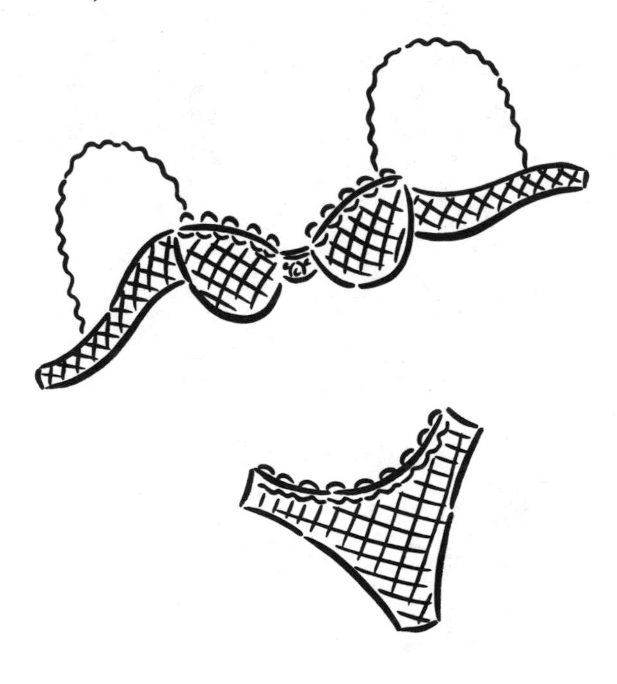

COMPILE a list of great date places with your friends. Give ratings for such features as best lighting, most romantic, most intimate, and best bathroom.

LEARN an alternative sport—blading, boarding, surfing. Then buy a cool piece of gear to get you motivated.

GO to your local train station to find out where you can go in a day: Head for the seashore in winter to walk on a deserted beach. Visit a museum in another town. Pick fruit on an old-fashioned farm.

BECOME an expert in something exotic that interests you: pearls, single malt scotch, orchids.

THE next time you go to a wedding, photograph your friends in black-and-white film. Make sure the pix are candid.

It is the friends that you can call up at 4:00 A.M. that matter.
—MARLENE DIETRICH

AFTER a bad day at work, hide from the world and treat yourself to a chamomile facial. Drape a thick terry towel over your head and place a bowl of steaming water and chamomile teabags below. Listen to Enya, breathe deeply, and relax for ten minutes. The flowery vapors will calm your soul while cleansing your complexion.

HOST a 70s party. All guests must come appropriately attired in polyester bell-bottoms or Pucci-style miniskirts. Decorate with love beads, lava lamps, and patchouli incense, and serve cheese fondue and Jell-O spiked with vodka. Here's the mandatory play list; make sure to end the night with slow-dancing to "Free Bird"!

"Dancing Queen" by Abba
"Beach Baby" by First Class
"Dim All the Lights" by Donna Summer
"Midnight Train to Georgia" by Gladys Knight and the Pips
Saturday Night Fever sound track
"Play That Funky Music" by Wild Cherry
"Get Down Tonight" by KC and the Sunshine Band
"I Will Survive" by Gloria Gaynor
"Kung Fu Fighting" by Carl Douglas
"December, 1963" by Frankie Valli
"Born to Be Alive" by Patrick Hernandez
"I Think I Love You" by The Partridge Family
"Daydream Believer" by The Monkees
"I Got You Babe" by Sonny and Cher
"Free Bird" by Lynyrd Skynyrd

SWISS CHEESE FONDUE

2 pounds Swiss cheese, grated
2 tablespoons flour
2 cups milk or white wine
1 teaspoon salt
¼ teaspoon white pepper
2 dashes nutmeg
French bread
Apples, cut into chunks

Mix the cheese and flour. Heat the milk or wine almost to boiling. Add the cheese slowly, stirring constantly. Season with salt, pepper, and nutmeg. When the mixture is almost at a boil, pour into a fondue pot and serve at once. Provide hunks of French bread and apples for dunking.

Makes 8 servings

JELL-O SHOTS

Follow the directions for making Jell-O, substituting vodka for the cold water. Pour into little paper cups and chill.

Serves its purpose

KEEP a goddess box. Inside put love letters, special postcards, photographs and magazine clippings, and mementos that make you feel good.

GROW herbs or hyacinth bulbs in a kitchen window box.

Be happy. It's just one way of being wise.

—COLETTE

PLAN a beat-the-blues Sunday night dinner every week with one friend or more. Take turns teaching each other how to cook favorite recipes. (The evening's noncooks can bring wine and clean up.)

PICK a sports team and become a die-hard fan.

DEEPEN your sense of the spiritual. Go to a religious service or sit in a cathedral alone for quiet reflection.

TAG along with a friend on a business trip. Order a decadent breakfast in bed after your pal has trudged off to work.

ON your first morning in a new city, wake up extra early and go for a walk or a jog. You'll see some sights and burn off last night's dessert.

SPEND one entire Sunday reading the paper from cover to cover (don't skip the editorials!).

TAKE out an insurance policy against all of life's indignities and disappointments: Learn how to make my friend Chuck's chocolate soufflé. One New Year's Eve, this exquisite concoction was a great pick-me-up before our various parties; in fact, it was so delicious that it didn't matter what else Amateur Night had in store. Here's the recipe:

A good cook is like a sorceress who dispenses happiness.

—ELSA SCHIAPARELLI

Chuck's Chocolate Soufflé

4 ounces bittersweet chocolate

1 cup heavy cream

5 eggs, separated

1 teaspoon vanilla extract

½ cup granulated sugar

Butter and freeze ramekins (soufflé dishes), 6 ½-cup to 1-cup size. Melt the chocolate and ½ cup of the cream. Whisk 3 yolks and ½ teaspoon of the vanilla into the chocolate. Beat 5 egg whites until foamy. Add ¼ cup of the granulated sugar. You can discard the 2 extra yolks. Rebutter the ramekins. Mix one-third of the egg whites into the chocolate. Fold the chocolate into the remaining egg whites just until blended.

Fill the ramekins two-thirds of the way. Bake on a cookie sheet at 425 degrees for 8 minutes.

While the soufflés are baking, whip the ½ cup of heavy cream with ¼ cup of sugar and ½ teaspoon vanilla. Dab a generous blob on each soufflé.

THE next time you are at a dinner party or on a car trip with friends, take turns casting the movie of your life. Start with the actress who would be best suited to play you and then pick the stars to play your friends, family, and (this is the hard part!) the man in your life. See how your version and those of your friends compare.

KEEP a travel diary by sending yourself a postcard every time you go away.

CALL in sick when you're not. Stay in bed, read the paper, and venture out for an early dinner at five.

PICK raspberries, strawberries, blueberries, and blackberries. Make a fruit shake—fun, healthy, delicious! Here's how:

Put 1 cup of sliced fruit, 8 ounces of skim milk, 1 tablespoon of sugar, and 2 ice cubes in a blender. Blend until the ice stops making that obnoxious loud noise. Sip with a straw and enjoy.

RESEARCH your dream vacation spot, using sources other than guidebooks and maps. For example, if your destination is the Florida Keys, read Hemingway and listen to Jimmy Buffet. If you've chosen Venice, watch Katharine Hepburn in *Summertime;* for Florence, read Henry James's *Portrait of a Lady.* Be creative: Ask previous visitors to recommend relevant books and movies, restaurants and bars, out-of-the-way places.

COLLECT small glass vases at garage sales or flea markets. Buy a dozen flowers and put a posy or two in each and line your windowsills with them.

MAKE a date with your past: Disconnect the phone, pour yourself a snifter of brandy, and reread your old love letters.

THE next time you share a weekend with the one you love, spend the first day doing whatever he wants, the second day doing whatever you want.

DURING your birthday month, buy all the fashion magazines you can and read your horoscopes.

STASH a big bottle of expensive perfume in your bottom desk drawer. Indulge in a aromatheraputic late-afternoon spray.

START a tradition with a faraway friend: Every year send each other a Christmas tree ornament.

BORROW someone's kids as an excuse for doing something *you* really want to do: Go to the zoo and feed the llamas, head for the beach to build sand castles, make a mess finger painting.

LEARN the proper way to clip, light, and smoke a cigar:

1. Use a cigar cutter to clip off the cap on the end. (Don't shave off more than the circumference of a pea, or you'll wind up spitting tobacco the whole time.)
2. Find someone handsome to light your cigar using a wooden—cedar is best—match. (You don't want to alter the taste of a fine cigar by flicking a Bic.) Hold the cigar above the flame so it lights by the heat rather than by the spark. Take deep draws without inhaling; to light the entire end, twirl the cigar between your fingertips.
3. When you are distracted by all the men who are now surrounding you, keep the cigar from extinguishing by taking strong enough pulls so that the end glows.
4. Don't tap the ash until it is just about to fall off.

SKINNY-DIP at least once a summer.

You will do foolish things, but do them with enthusiasm.

—COLETTE

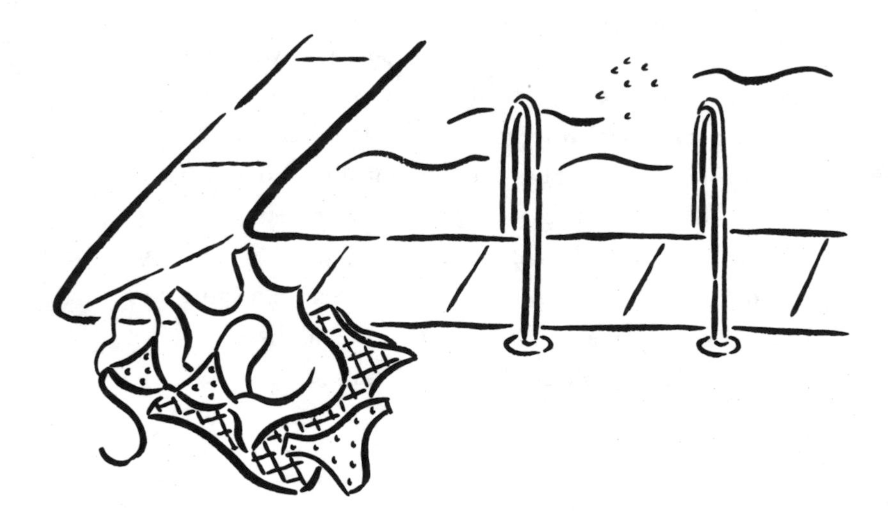

SLATHER on peppermint foot cream or, if possible, persuade someone else to do it for you. Air-dry and then slip on white cotton socks to wear to sleep. Wake up with silky soft tic-tac-toes.

BLOW-DRY your hair while riding on the back of a motorcycle.

Life is either a daring adventure or nothing at all.
—HELEN KELLER

GO window shopping with a friend after the stores have closed. Pick out your favorite items in the displays.

RENT your all-time favorite movie with a new friend or boyfriend. Indulge in retro treats: Milk Duds, popcorn drenched in real butter, and non-diet soda.

ON a rainy, miserable day, go for a walk on a waterfront. Feel very Heathcliffish and enjoy the fact that fewer people are outside.

SPEND an afternoon with a parent or grandparent going through family photos. Get to know your ancestors, and weave old lore into new relationships.

RECIPE for a perfect fall day: Put on your favorite flannel shirt and head outside to check out the foliage. Rake some leaves just long enough to work up an appetite for my friend Kristin's Killer Apple Krisp. (Warning: Don't try this recipe without several pints of vanilla Häagen-Dazs in the freezer.)

KRISTIN'S KILLER APPLE KRISP

4 cups peeled, cored, sliced Granny Smith, Jonathan, or Macintosh apples
1 teaspoon ground cinnamon
1 teaspoon salt
1 cup water
1 cup flour, sifted
1 cup sugar
1 tablespoon butter
vanilla ice cream (preferably high-fat)

First, put on your favorite Van Morrison CD. Arrange the apple slices in a buttered 10 by 6 by 2-inch baking pan. Sprinkle with the cinnamon, salt, and water. Combine the flour, sugar, and butter with a pastry cutter. Mix until the consistency of coarse meal. Sprinkle the mixture over the apples. Bake in a preheated 350-degree oven for 40 minutes. Serve warm in front of a fire, with enough ice cream to induce a proper sugar coma.

GET rid of every single pair of uncomfortable shoes (new or old) in your closet.

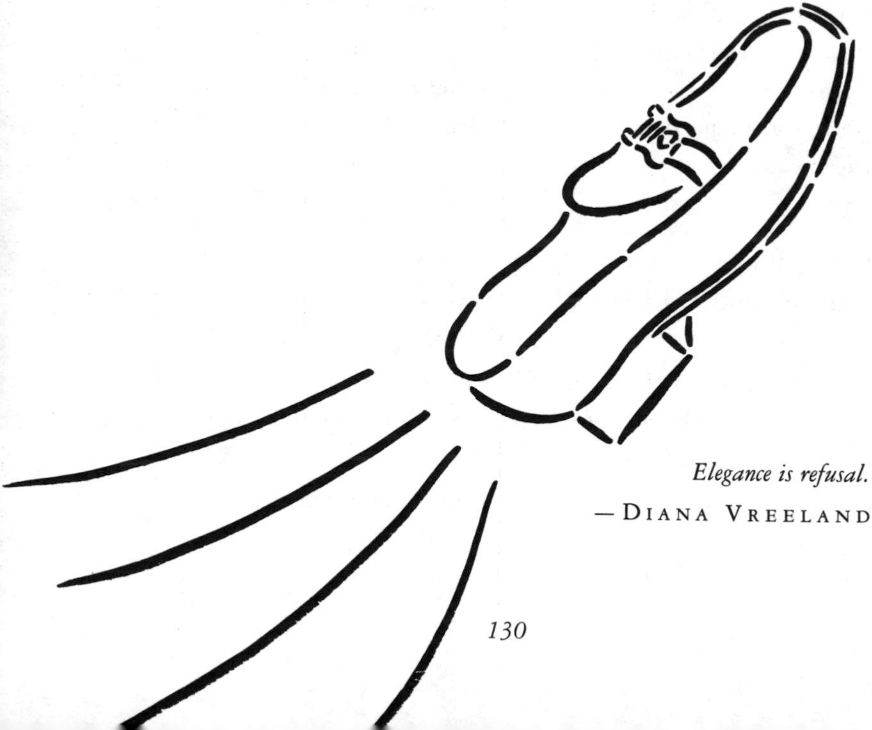

Elegance is refusal.
—DIANA VREELAND

THROW out the bathroom scale.

ON a rainy afternoon, have an Audrey Hepburn film festival. Must rents: *Breakfast at Tiffany's, Roman Holiday,* and *Two for the Road.*

IN the winter, put flannel sheets on your bed, open the windows, and sleep naked with the one you love. Share your warmth.

DRIVE with the car radio blasting and sing at the top of your lungs. Don't stop when you approach the tolls.

To travel hopefully is a better thing than to arrive.
—ROBERT LOUIS STEVENSON

IN the summer, put sprigs of mint and blueberries in your ice trays—great for ice tea and lemonade! Serve in large frosted glasses stowed in your freezer door. As you sip, pretend you are resting on a shady Victorian porch. (If you happen to own one, all the better!)

HAVE a standing date with a friend to frequent flea markets on a weekend morning. Scour the rows for antique cocktail shakers or sterling silver napkin rings with posh names engraved on them. Have dinner parties and imagine what these people were like.

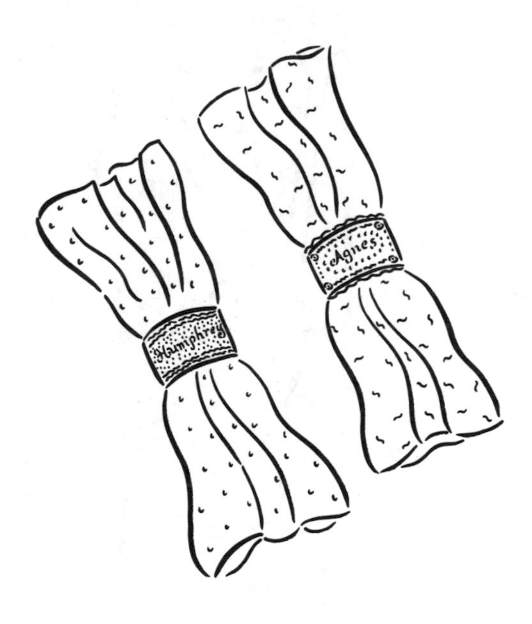

REREAD Kay Thompson's *Eloise.* Go to the Plaza hotel and act like her.

BEFORE falling asleep at night, be thankful for three things, large or small, in your day or your life.

Light tomorrow with today!

—ELIZABETH BARRETT BROWNING

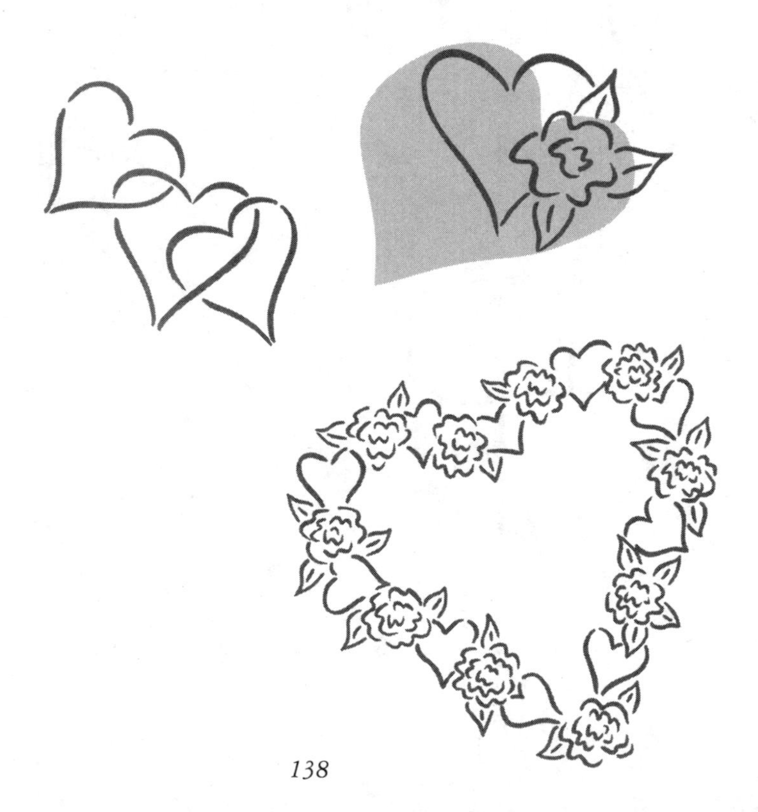

BUY yourself a sumptuous bouquet of your favorite flowers. Every time you notice them, remind yourself that they are from someone special.

ACKNOWLEDGMENTS

This book would not exist without my "finders": my dear friend and editor, Hilary Black, and my agent, Claudia Cross. Both turned the work of the publishing process into play. Thanks also to Melanie Parks, for bringing my ideas to life. The book wrote itself, thanks to my friends and their selfless, guerrilla-style research over the years. The correspondents include: Susan Sobocinski for the late-night, naughty shift; Isobel Coleman for teaching me the definition of sybaritic; Laura Quill for belly laughs gift-wrapped in brown paper bags: Michael Pearson for being my best "boy" friend; Mary Castellone for being the Lovely Rhythm Queen; Meredith Berkman, my narashkite police commissioner; Rebecca Ascher-Walsh, my own personal Robin Leach; Holly Millea and Virginia de Liagre for being girly-whirlies; Kristin Starr, for the best rolls before, during, and after cooking class; and Karen Finneran, my most constant copilot in the pursuit of fun. The biggest thanks of all go to the Scarlotti family for raising me never to take anything seriously—except, of course, having a good time.

About the Author

Melina Gerosa is the Senior Entertainment Editor at *Ladies' Home Journal,* where she has profiled Oprah Winfrey, Julia Roberts, Rosie O'Donnell, and Mel Gibson among others. She began her career in fun growing up in Larchmont, New York, and perfected it at Boston College, where she majored in English and art and minored in procrastination. Gerosa currently lives in New York City, where she enjoys sipping martinis, smoking cigars, and shopping in stores she can't really afford. A freelance writer for *Glamour, Cosmopolitan, Mademoiselle,* and *Entertainment Weekly* magazines, she is at work on the screenplay for a romantic comedy.